No doubt you've been bombarded with "expert" advice from your parents, professors, and countless advisors. It's time you got advice you can really use— from fellow students who've been where you're headed.

All **Students Helping Students™** guides are written and edited by top students and recent grads from colleges and universities across the U.S. You'll find no preachy or condescending advice here—just stuff to help you succeed in tackling your academic, social, and professional challenges.

Check out these other **Students Helping Students™** titles at your local or college bookstore, and online at Amazon.com, BN.com, Borders.com, and other book retailers!

Each one is packed with practical and useful advice from people who really know what they're talking about—**fellow students who've been where you're headed!**

GETTING THE MOST
FROM STUDY ABROAD

Don't sign up for a study abroad program without checking out this guide filled with tips on figuring out where and when to go, how to deal with culture shock and host family dynamics, how to choose the best classes and find local treasures, and, most of all, how to truly immerse yourself in your new culture. Study abroad can be the best time of your life—pick up this guide to help you make sure that it is. *($6.95)*

FISHING
FOR A MAJOR

You might know exactly what you want to do with your life. Or you might have no idea at all. In either case, reading what other students think about finding a major that makes you happy can help you consider things you've not thought of. Find out how other students approach choosing classes, getting the best of the advising system, thinking about a career and finding a passion—and you might discover more than just a college major. *($6.95)*

SCORING A
GREAT INTERNSHIP

Finding and getting a killer internship during college has no downside— you'll learn a ton, spice up your resume, meet new people, and hopefully get a few steps closer to knowing what you'd like to do with your life after college. This guide is packed with tips on how to find the best internships, get yourself noticed and accepted, and how to learn the most once you're there. *($6.95)*

To learn more about **Students Helping Students™**
guides, read samples, share your own experiences with
other students, suggest a topic or ask questions, visit us at
www.studentshelpingstudents.com!

Students Helping Students™

TACKLING YOUR FIRST COLLEGE PAPER

First Edition

NATAVI GUIDES

New York

Tackling Your First College Paper.
First Edition.

Published by **NATAVI GUIDES**. For information on bulk purchases or custom promotional guides, please contact the publisher via email at sales@nataviguides.com or 1.866.425.4218. You can learn more about our promotional guides program on our website, www.nataviguides.com.

Printed in the U.S.A.

ISBN 0-9719392-7-6

Library of Congress Cataloging-in-Publication Data

Tackling your first college paper.-- 1st ed.
    p. cm. -- (Students helping students)
  ISBN 0-9719392-7-6 (pbk. : alk. paper)
  1. English language--Rhetoric--Handbooks, manuals, etc. 2. Report writing--Handbooks, manuals, etc. I. Natavi Guides (Firm) II. Series.
  PE1408 .T14 2002
  808'.042--dc21

                              2002011789

Students Helping Students™
"same pager"

Before you dive into reading this guide, we'd like to share with you a bit of the philosophy on which it's based. We figure that you'll find it more useful if we're on the same page as you begin.

We think that you're pretty smart and savvy and don't like people talking down to you.

We know that you have lots to do and are interested in reading only the most relevant information.

We believe that you appreciate the value of advice given by someone who has been where you're going.

And one more thing: Don't just read this guide. <u>USE IT</u> to help you get where you're going. Write in it and on it, fold pages you find useful and refer to them later, carry it in your bag for good luck. Do whatever it is that will help you tackle the tasks before you!

the primary author

Scott Grinsell is a junior at Williams College, where he plans to major in history. At Williams, Scott is a representative on the College Council, a Junior Advisor, and the coordinator of a tutoring program for at-risk high school students. As a freshman, he was nominated by one of his professors to be a tutor in the Writing Workshop.

Scott has won numerous awards for his writing, but they're all from his mom.

the contributors

Students from Carleton College, Columbia University, Cornell University, Haverford College, Middlebury College, Northwestern University, the University of Pennsylvania, Wesleyan University, and Vassar College contributed to this guide.

author's note

My stereo was blasting, and my window was open to let the smell of dirty clothes waft out of my room. I had my name at the top of the page, and the cursor was blinking, waiting anxiously for me to start writing. I had nothing to say about Plato's *Republic* and about ten hours to say it. It was after midnight. I knew I was in over my head. Even the cursor knew it.

For me, writing my first college paper did not go as planned. I didn't start outlining the week before it was due. I didn't even read the question until the day before. I didn't know what to expect or where to begin. I wrote most of it in a bleary-eyed daze. Plato was certainly not impressed.

Even though most of us wrote papers in high school, writing the first few papers in college can be very intimidating. Writing might not have been your best friend in high school. You might not be sure about what your professor expects from you. The topic might seem too broad. Or maybe you're just overwhelmed with college in general.

Try to relax. A college paper is a chance to be creative and say something interesting about the material in class. You don't need to write something worthy of publication in a journal or a book. And your paper certainly doesn't have to be the best one you'll ever write.

I hope this guide gives you a feeling of confidence as you start writing. We've tried to break down the process of writing a paper into digestible bites and to point out a few tips to make your task easier. By the time you finish reading you'll be able to plan and write a great paper without losing sleep—or at least not all of it!

contents

what it is
2
what it's not
3
getting started
4
developing a topic and a thesis
12
making a plan
25
writing your paper
36
revising and editing your paper
54
approaching a research paper
66
the daily grind
77
what "they" say
80
helpful resources
82
the final word
85

what it is

A college paper is a short piece of writing that makes a claim and sustains an argument supporting it. A typical paper assignment in the humanities can range anywhere from a one-page response to thirty pages of original research. The first few papers you write in college will probably be between one and ten pages.

It's unlikely that your first paper will involve much research. In most first-year courses, professors will probably ask you to write about materials you've covered in class. In this guide, we've assumed that you're writing a paper based on course materials, but we've also included a section that gives some advice about approaching papers based on independent research.

However long the assignment is, your paper must have a main point—the infamous thesis. Your high school English teachers probably insisted that your papers have theses, and you're probably used to writing short papers that make a central claim. A thesis gives a paper focus and makes it a piece of academic writing.

A paper also needs evidence supporting the thesis. You might have been able to trick a few high school teachers by skillfully repeating your thesis in different ways for two or three pages. College professors won't be fooled as easily. They want to know why your thesis is valid, and you should show this by using supporting arguments and evidence.

Your college papers will allow you to be much more flexible and creative than your high school assignments, and while writing your first few papers can be intimidating, you'll have much more control over how and what you write in them.

what it's not

Your first college paper is not the final test of your intellectual abilities. It won't get you into the honor society and it won't lock you out. It won't even determine how well you do in the class you write it for. The first paper you write in college is an experiment. It's a chance to try new approaches and work on your writing. It's a first step, not a final exam.

Try to keep in mind that you'll probably write dozens of papers in college. Each time you sit down to write, you'll have better intuition about how to organize your paper and a better feeling for language and style. Your writing will improve organically as you read more, interact with your professors, and hear their comments on your writing.

A college paper is not a five-paragraph essay. Many of the papers you wrote in high school might have fit one standard format—a one-paragraph introduction plus three supporting paragraphs plus a conclusion. College papers tend to be more complex in their structure and vary significantly by discipline. You'll have to be more flexible and more creative in your approach.

A college paper is not a doctoral dissertation, nor is it a senior thesis. You don't need to forge new academic territory or say anything terribly profound. You do need to make a strong case supporting and analyzing a particular thesis, and do it through clear and error-free writing.

getting started

It's useful to think of your paper as the culmination of your experience in a particular class. All of your reading, all of your time in class, and all of the hours you spend thinking about the course materials will be part of your paper— either directly or by providing you with relevant background. If you learn a ton about a certain subject— whether it's early American poetry or the sociology of Japanese cell phone use—you'll be able to draw on that material when you write your paper.

To that end, absorbing as much as you can from your classes will actually help you write better papers—and get better grades. Don't skip too many lectures, take notes, pay attention to your professor's preferences, and try to do at least some of each week's reading. When time comes to write a paper, you'll be in great shape.

GET INVOLVED IN YOUR CLASSES

▼

TAKE NOTES

▼

DO THE READING . . . AT LEAST SOMETIMES

▼

KNOW WHAT YOUR PROFESSORS WANT

▼

PLAN AHEAD

GET INVOLVED IN YOUR CLASSES

Not every college class is interesting, many are scheduled way too early in the morning, and some are taught by professors who care extremely little about teaching. All of that—combined with the fact that you're pretty overwhelmed with academics, extracurriculars, your roommate's music-blasting, and oh, that tempting sound of fun down the hall—can serve as a great excuse to skip class.

Try not to give into the temptation too often. You'll be wasting your tuition money and your college time, but more practically, you'll be missing out on a lot of learning that can help you ace your papers and exams.

If your class has a discussion component, try to participate as much as possible. When something comes to mind and it seems appropriate, don't hesitate to raise your hand and say it. Some of the best paper topics come out of these kinds of informal exchanges in class, where one student proposes an interpretation and the professor and other students comment on it.

Even if you don't have an opportunity to participate out loud, try to really think about the material during class. If you're sitting at the back of a dark lecture hall, it might be tempting to just sit back and write down what the professor says. Try to think of ways that you might challenge your professor's ideas, and write down questions that come to mind. Your question might later lead to a paper topic or might make you think of something else that does.

TAKE NOTES

You might have been able to get through high school without taking notes. You may not think of yourself as the note-taking type. You may not even own a notebook.

Get one. Taking notes can make writing papers much easier because you'll have a summary of what was covered in class and what core issues you might want to discuss in your paper. Many professors use class time to emphasize what parts of the material they consider the most important for you to learn. Write those down. You'll want to make sure to touch on these points when you write your paper.

There are so many ways to take notes and you probably have one that works for you already. Some people meticulously outline each major point covered in class; others find it quite sufficient to write down a few brief words or phrases. Do what works for you and don't worry about what you should be doing. The key is to write down just enough to jar your memory later on when you look over your notes.

What you shouldn't do is try to write down every word that comes out of your professor's mouth. None of us can write and listen well at the same time and you don't want to miss what's going on in class because you're too busy highlighting in your notebook. Write down the main ideas and make sure that you write legibly enough to make sense of your notes later. Use stars, arrows, circles, funny faces, and exclamation points—whatever works for you—to emphasize particularly important details.

DO THE READING . . . AT LEAST SOMETIMES

"More than anything else, doing your reading is essential to writing a good paper. Not just doing the reading, but doing it critically and extracting the main ideas from it. This will really help you when you're trying to think of a good topic or thesis."

**History major,
Cornell University '04**

When you're in a class based primarily on papers, the more you read, the more options you'll have for paper topics. Say, for example, you're taking a class on medieval Bavarian literature. The more you've read about medieval Bavaria, the better intuition you'll have about the topic, and the more things you'll have to say about it. Even if you don't write a paper about every Bavarian poem you read, each poem will add to your intuitive grasp of Bavarian literature. When you write your paper about the symbolism of beer steins (mugs) in Medieval Bavarian epics, you'll be more confident and better informed.

Of course, you don't have to read every paragraph of every book or article that your professor assigns. We've all had a few professors who think it's important to read every page of a book when only two chapters are relevant to the course. The idea here is to skim through the material and try to judge what parts are most relevant to the core of what you're learning in class. One way to do this is to read the first few paragraphs of each chapter or section.

Another great guide to what and how much you should read is your professor—pay attention to what points he or she emphasizes in class and make sure to read up on those.

In general, it's a good idea to do most of the reading at the beginning on each semester. That way, you'll learn what you need to read carefully and what, if anything, you can skim or skip completely.

If you know what the majority of your class reading covers you'll have much more flexibility when choosing your paper topic and enough background to structure your initial arguments and ideas. This will really help. You want to avoid having to read huge chunks of class material for the first time after your paper is assigned.

> *"Before I even begin to sit down to write my outline I always make sure I've read all the relevant sources, underlined and dog-eared important pages, and generally understood the ideas of the texts."*
>
> **Philosophy and Computer Science major,**
> **Vassar College '04**

KNOW WHAT YOUR PROFESSORS WANT

Besides the obvious benefits of getting to know some pretty smart people, knowing your professors can help you write better papers and get higher grades. Professors are people with personal tastes. Each has subjective preferences and quirks. Get to know what these are and don't ignore them in your papers. While a solid, clear-written paper will fare well in most classes, understanding what your particular professor is looking for can also help.

Some professors obsess about students sticking extremely close to assigned topics and class material. Others want you to extrapolate from specific topics to broader issues. The better you know your professor's preferences—read "requirements"—the more you'll know about shaping your paper.

Go to your professor's office hours. Talk about the class, the paper topic, what questions you have, and what ideas you might like to explore. Ask your professor about his or her interests—listening to how your professor talks about books, articles, or even other papers can reveal quite a bit about what he or she might expect from you in class. And don't worry about imposing—most professors appreciate when students show interest in their class.

PLAN AHEAD

It's a pretty good idea to start working on your paper as soon as possible, especially if you're a bit anxious about it. You don't need to churn out ten drafts before the paper is due, but you should keep the due date in mind when you receive your class syllabus.

In many courses, you may not be able to start your paper very far in advance, mostly because you won't have done the reading necessary to answer your professor's question. Usually, your professor will give you paper topics about a week or two in advance of when the paper is due. When you get the assignment, make a plan for how you'll tackle it—and keep in mind what other deadlines you have for other classes.

You might find it helpful to put together a brief timeline. Set a few rough dates for figuring out your topic and thesis, sketching your outline, writing your first draft, and finishing your revisions.

As you'll probably find, however, writing doesn't always happen on a schedule. You may encounter problems in your first draft that you hadn't initially expected, or you may have a harder time resisting the lure of throwing around a frisbee on the sunny quad lawn. If you make a timeline, give yourself some flexibility. Instead of holding yourself rigidly to the dates that you initially set, use them as indicators. If a certain step of the process takes you a bit longer than you planned, you'll be able to judge how much time you have left to get the rest done.

developing a topic and a thesis

In high school, choosing a paper topic probably wasn't something you thought about very much. If you read <u>Moby Dick</u> in your English class, then you had to write a paper on it in response to a specific question from your teacher. In college, courses tend to move much faster and cover a much wider range of material. As a result, you'll often have the ability to choose what you write about.

Once you find a topic, the challenge is finding something to argue about it. Carefully think about what your paper will say at the beginning of the process and it will help you write more clearly as you develop your argument and analysis. All good papers begin with an original and interesting idea that becomes the paper's thesis—the main point that you'll present to the reader.

AIM FOR A CLEAR AND SPECIFIC TOPIC
▼

DON'T CHOOSE IN ISOLATION
▼

WRITE ABOUT SOMETHING INTERESTING
▼

MOVE FROM TOPIC TO THESIS
▼

FREE-WRITE OR BRAINSTORM IF YOU GET STUCK
▼

EVALUATE YOUR THESIS
▼

DON'T GET TOO ATTACHED TO YOUR THESIS

AIM FOR A CLEAR AND SPECIFIC TOPIC

Assuming that you have a choice about your topic, you'll probably either be asked to select one from a list of assigned topics or questions, or be given free reign to come up with one of your own. For first-year seminars and introductory level classes, it's pretty common to receive a list of possible topics to which you can add with permission from the professor.

Take a few minutes to read through the list of topics your professor hands out and see what comes to mind. Jot down a few ideas about each one, and think about which interests you the most. It helps to look through some of your class notes or materials to jar your memory—especially if some of the topics deal with material you covered a few weeks back. There's no need to re-read everything you might use. Just skim through what you think is important.

Your paper topic should be very clear and you should know exactly what you're writing about. Try this: See if you can summarize your topic in a single sentence. If not, rethink it and see if you need to reduce the scope or choose a better-organized central theme.

Your topic should also be pretty specific. Unless you're asked to synthesize or summarize all of the material you've covered—ouch!—you shouldn't try to write a paper about everything you've learned in class. Pick one idea, one historical period, one book, one theme, two things or concepts to compare, or a particular theory—but do pick and don't drive yourself crazy by trying to include everything.

Choosing your own topic can sometimes be a lot more difficult than choosing from a list of assigned topics. You have a blank canvas in front of you and you have to figure out how to fill it. Don't panic. A good way to think of topics is to go through some of the class material you found particularly interesting and ask questions about it.

Take our Bavarian literature class as an example. A few questions you could consider are:

• What are some prevalent themes in Bavarian poetry?

• What are some similarities between Bavarian poetry and the poetry of other countries?

• How are historical events reflected in Bavarian literature?

Your answers to broad questions like these can become valid topics. For example, you might end up writing about the symbolism of beer steins in Bavarian poetry.

When thinking about your topic, consider the number of pages that you have to fill. If you're writing a three-page paper, maybe you shouldn't write a comparison of five artistic movements or ideas. Try starting with two.

Some people like to choose the topic they think is the "hardest," but this is quite silly. There isn't a clearly defined set of criteria that identify certain topics as the "hardest" and most professors try to make paper topics similar in scope and depth. By trying to choose the most difficult topic you risk missing out on writing about something that genuinely interests you and has a much greater chance of producing a great paper.

Don't worry if you can't choose a topic right away. Sometimes the best ideas for papers will come at breakfast between bites of a Pop Tart. Give your thoughts some time to percolate.

DON'T CHOOSE IN ISOLATION

You don't have to figure out your paper topic all on your own. Talk to your class T.A. and spend a few minutes discussing your topic with your professor. You'll find that these discussions are most useful when you already have a few ideas about your topic and are looking for more specific feedback than the answer to the question: "What do you think I should write about?"

Try to take your professor's suggestions to heart, especially if he or she thinks that your topic is too broad in scope. Professors have seen more than a few students try to take on a topic for a five-page paper that is more suitable for a book. Get some advice and you'll save yourself frustration later on.

WRITE ABOUT SOMETHING INTERESTING

As you think about possible books, authors, or issues to write about, try to pick something you find interesting. If you don't care at all about your topic, the hours you spend at the keyboard or in the library will be unnecessarily painful. And you're much more likely to write a great paper and do well if you're writing about something that you find at least moderately interesting.

The wonderful thing about college is that you can usually choose what you write about, even if you have to choose from a list. Take advantage of that. Each topic can be approached in a dozen different ways and you should be able to find a way that interests you the most.

Think about it this way: You have to write the paper anyway, so why not be interested in what you're writing about.

"You'll always write better when you're interested in what you're writing, interested in learning about the topic, and interested in explaining it to others. Try to find a topic that really brings into focus the crux of the subject matter or the course. Writing about

myths about George Washington's false teeth may sound more interesting to research, but you'll get more out of that American history class—and you'll find more relevant material—if you write about his relationship with the other founders."

**Journalism and Political Science major,
Northwestern University '04**

MOVE FROM TOPIC TO THESIS

Once you've picked a general topic for your paper, you need to come up with a thesis. Your thesis is the main and focal point of your paper and it's the position you'll take on your particular topic.

A good way to move from a topic to a thesis is to try to rephrase your topic as a question. For example, if you're writing about beer steins in a Bavarian poem, you might ask: "What is the meaning of the beer steins in this Bavarian poem?"

Your answer to the question may very well be your thesis: "The beer steins serve as a symbol for masculine insecurity."

A thesis is a claim that you can argue for or against. It should be something that you can present persuasively and clearly in the scope of your paper, so keep in mind the page count. If possible, your thesis should also be somewhat original.

"Your thesis should make an analytical argument. That is, it should go beyond summary. To make sure this is the case, you should ask yourself whether someone could contend that your thesis is wrong. If so, you have succeeded in proposing an analytical argument."

**Astronomy major,
Columbia University '04**

To give you a better idea, here are some examples of not-so-great theses:

- Germany lost World War II.

- <u>Crime and Punishment</u> is about death.

- Is the Cold War really over?

One is a fact, one is a half-baked interpretation, and one is a question. All of them have an element that sounds vaguely thesis-like, but they all fall short of being real theses. The first statement isn't really controversial and you can't make a great argument about it. The second is too vague and needs a bit more focus. The third statement doesn't make a claim, but asks a question. It's a first step to a thesis, but it's not one yet.

All of these statements have the kernel of an idea. To turn them into theses, it's important to add a touch of justification and explanation. For example, "Germany lost World War II because Hitler's expansionist vision spiraled out of control toward the end of the war." This could be a thesis. It makes a point that can be argued for and against, and it's one that can be reasonably supported with evidence.

FREE-WRITE OR BRAINSTORM IF YOU GET STUCK

We all get stuck from time to time. If you can't think of a thesis, it sometimes helps to open up your word processor—or a notebook—and start writing about a topic until you have something resembling an argument. Burn some incense, slip on your Birkenstock sandals, and let the intellectual juices flow. Don't worry about style or structure. Just try to get some ideas down on paper.

See where this process takes you. Usually, after a page or two, you'll have a clearer idea of what you want to write about. Press print, and scan through the pages to see where you might have come to a thesis. When you find it, circle it. Rephrase it, if necessary, to make it sound clearer and more specific. (Refer to the previous section for some general thesis guidelines.)

Another way to develop a thesis without actually writing full pages of text is to pull out some scratch paper and start scribbling down whatever words and concepts come to mind about your topic. Don't worry about them making sense initially. Get a few concepts and ideas down on paper and then read over them to see if any can evolve into a thesis.

Free-writing and brainstorming are great ways to get you thinking and get your mind out of a temporary warp. Give them a shot and try not to worry about spending this extra time—if you don't have a strong thesis, your paper will suffer and you'll have a hard time writing it.

EVALUATE YOUR THESIS

"Try not to write for the grade. Ask yourself, can people read this paper and feel like they learned something? Try to say something that isn't obvious."

Independent Major in Social Policy and Theory, Haverford College '04

Once you have a rough idea of your thesis, take a few minutes and test it out. That way, you won't write three pages and realize that it's flawed or misguided. Here are a few ways to make sure that your thesis will help lead to a strong argument and a well-structured paper:

- Read your thesis out loud. Does it make sense to you? Does it make clear what your main point is? Remember, you can argue for or against your thesis, but the reader of your paper should be able to know your position as soon as he or she reads your thesis statement.

- Show your thesis statement to a few of your friends who aren't taking your class and ask them if it makes sense. Do they understand what it means, or do they look like Bambi caught in the headlights of an eighteen-wheeler? Your thesis should make sense even to someone who knows nothing about your class, so consider your friends' reactions carefully.

- Does your thesis answer all parts of your professor's question? If you have an assigned topic, it's critical that you tackle the entire issue in the way that you're asked to. If the question asks you to "explain the most important causes and effects of the fall of the Soviet Union," your thesis needs to address both the causes and the effects.

- Check the scope of your thesis. Are you trying to argue something that can be argued in the required length of your paper or are you taking on the history of the world in five pages?

- Is your thesis controversial just for the sake of being controversial? It's fantastic if you have an original idea, but make sure that your thesis isn't simply absurd. In high school, some of your teachers might have given you a good grade for taking a contrary position, just because it had some element of originality. College professors probably won't be that generous. Most of them have spent more years than you have been alive thinking about their subjects, and they can tell the difference between a thesis that is trying to be "out there" and one that is genuinely original. Having a unique thesis is great, but you still have to make sure that you can reasonably argue it in your paper.

"Try very hard to make your thesis as direct, coherent, and well-written as possible. Having a clear thesis is not just important for the reader to understand your paper; it's also important to make sure you have a complete understanding of what it is you want to say."

Philosophy and Computer Science major, Vassar College '04

DON'T GET TOO ATTACHED TO YOUR THESIS

Regardless of how hard you work to come up with a strong, clear, and original thesis, chances are that it will change at least somewhat before you're done with your paper. As you get more involved with your topic and the specifics of each part of your arguments, you'll probably come up with some ideas and conclusions that are different from your original thesis.

That happens a lot, so try not to get frustrated. Part of the reason professors make us write papers is to force us to think about the class material in depth. And when we think about something for a long time, we're bound to change our initial position or opinion. As you write your paper, always refer back to your original thesis and see if you still think it's valid. If you need to tweak it a bit, do it. Just because you initially thought it was a great thesis doesn't mean you have to stick to it.

topic and thesis notes

making a plan

Now that you have a good thesis, you need to come up with analyses and arguments to support it. You probably already have some idea of where you want to go with your paper, but you might find it helpful to pause and make a brief outline of your main points and arguments. Even if you're rushed for time, take a few minutes to think about the layout and organization of your paper. Knowing where your paper is headed will help you when you actually begin to write it.

ORGANIZE YOUR MATERIALS
▼

MAKE A ROUGH OUTLINE
▼

CONCENTRATE ON YOUR THESIS
▼

DON'T IGNORE COUNTER-ARGUMENTS
▼

DON'T TAKE YOUR OUTLINE TOO SERIOUSLY
▼

TALK TO YOUR PROFESSOR

ORGANIZE YOUR MATERIALS

When you start developing an overall plan for your paper, surround yourself with your books and notes from class. This sounds obvious, but it's easy to write an entire outline for a paper without ever walking across your dorm room to pull a few books off the shelf.

Have access to books that are related to your topic even if you don't plan to specifically use them in your paper. Sometimes as you're writing your outline, you may decide to revise your thesis to include another source. You may find that a thoughtful comparison with another work, even if it's only one sentence long, can illuminate your entire argument.

If you're surrounded by materials from class, you'll also get into the right mindset for thinking about your paper. Simply being immersed in your class notes will get you thinking about the subject as a whole and help you come with up with ideas for your paper.

MAKE A ROUGH OUTLINE

"I find it helpful to first take notes on everything I think might be a relevant fact or quote in a book. Then I compile all of my notes from all of my sources and categorize each one. For example, 'background,' 'point A,' or 'related to B and C.' Then I prioritize and order just those category titles—if there are a lot, some may be subsections of another—and then I've got a great start to a coherent outline."

Journalism and Political Science major, Northwestern University '04

None of us probably got through high school without writing at least a few detailed outlines, especially for research papers. It's not a bad idea to have an outline, but it doesn't have to be long or very formal. Its main goal is to serve as the roadmap for your paper, to capture the overall structure and flow of your main points and arguments.

Start by writing your thesis at the top of the page—the point of the outline is to find a layout for your paper that most effectively argues your thesis. Look at the phrasing of your thesis and your professor's question. Is there a structure implicit in either one? Does it make sense to write about the overall structure of *Hamlet* before you start writing about the specific language structures? Try to find an organization that develops naturally from your thesis.

Think in terms of sections before you start thinking in terms of paragraphs. In high school, your thesis could probably be supported in one section. Each paragraph focused on one piece of supporting evidence that related directly to your thesis. Your theses for papers in college will often have multiple parts. Each section of your paper will probably contain a few paragraphs, which support a part of your thesis. Not all papers will break down into multiple sections, but most of them will work out that way.

author's corner
▾

I tend to use a different outlining method depending on what kind of paper I'm writing, and how comfortable I am with the topic. Sometimes, when I'm writing a compare and contrast paper, I find it helpful to sketch a large chart with each item as a column, and each subtopic as a row.

If I'm writing a more free-flowing argument, I sometimes write a very rough prose outline with no formal structure. I'll write a word or two for things I know a lot about, and write more for areas that I still want to think about. I find that this combination of free-writing and outlining is a great way to refine my thesis and develop language to use in my first draft.
▲

Don't obsess about outlining every paragraph and getting down every detail. You'll drive yourself crazy and spend time writing in your outline what you should be writing in your paper. And if you get too bogged down in details you'll risk losing track of the overall flow of your paper. Instead, write down your main arguments and ideas in an order that makes them most powerful, and then fill in the details when you actually begin to write.

There's always a question about how to order your main arguments to make them most effective. There's no science to determine this and you should rely on your logic and intuition to figure it out. Keep in mind that people remember what they read first and last better than what they read in the middle, so you might want to put your strongest argument either at the beginning or the end of your paper.

Once you have the overall structure of your paper laid out, you can think about what each of the smaller sections might contain. Jot down a few notes for each, indicating to yourself what specific points you'll want to cover.

Check out the simple outline template on the next page. It's not rocket science, but it might help you lay out your thoughts and get organized. Feel free to write in it or create a new one to fill in.

SAMPLE OUTLINE TEMPLATE

Here's a template that you can use to structure your outline. Adapt it to your particular needs and use it to help you focus your research and writing.

Overall Topic

Thesis Statement

Supporting Argument #1

- Main evidence (a)
- Main evidence (b)

Supporting Argument #2

- Main evidence (a)
- Main evidence (b)

Supporting Argument #3

- Main evidence (a)
- Main evidence (b)

CONCENTRATE ON YOUR THESIS

Remember that all of this planning and outlining you're doing is for a reason: You want to organize your paper in a way that most effectively presents and argues your thesis statement. Take a look at your brief outline and see if you've accomplished this.

- Do your main arguments sound convincing?

- Do they address your main thesis?

- Are your arguments presented in the most persuasive order?

- Can you argue them reasonably well with the information from your class materials?

DON'T IGNORE COUNTER-ARGUMENTS

As you write your outline, consider possible objections to your arguments and your thesis. If someone reading your paper disagreed with your thesis, what would they say? How would they respond to the arguments you're making?

The best and most persuasive papers take on counter-arguments in the open rather than ignoring them or just mentioning them in passing. There are very few, if any, arguments in the world that cannot be argued against.

Think about counter-arguments to your thesis and use them in your paper to make it stronger and more balanced.

You can fit counter-arguments into your paper in different ways. You can group them together in one section or you can discuss each of them in the section of your paper where each is most relevant. Think about your topic and your thesis and see which option works best.

Don't just acknowledge that there are points of view that disagree with your arguments. Explore each counter-argument in the context of your topic and explain why your thesis is still valid even though this particular counter-argument exists. Is the counter-argument weak? Invalid? Valid but not relevant to your particular thesis? Find what makes the counter-argument weaker than your own argument and explain this in your paper.

DON'T TAKE YOUR OUTLINE TOO SERIOUSLY

"If you use your outline too carefully, your paper can become overly choppy. Try to be flexible."

**History major,
Cornell University '04**

Try to avoid thinking of your outline as a precise plan for your paper. It's more like an artist's sketch than an architect's blueprint. An outline is supposed to give you a sense of where you're going, but it shouldn't include every step along the way. As you write, you'll probably discover new issues you want to address and decide that there are some things you can leave out. When you revise your paper, you may end up deleting entire paragraphs or whole sections. Allow yourself the flexibility to do this and avoid being stifled by your own outline.

author's corner
▼

I try to avoid even looking at my outline all the time as I write most of my papers. Sometimes, I'll even turn it over as I write so that I'm not tempted to copy whole sentences or phrases from it.

If a paper has a complex and formal structure with lots of parts, I use an outline to keep track of all of my arguments and counter-arguments. But even for papers like that, I try to keep my outline as a reference tool rather than something that dictates my paper.

▲

Some students actually choose not to write outlines at all because they don't want to feel confined by a predefined plan. (Or maybe because they just don't want to bother.) You might be one of those people, and if you feel that you can handle your paper without an outline, you should trust your instincts. Our only suggestion is that you try it once, that you don't make it too detailed and overbearing, and that you see if it makes your life easier. It might.

TALK TO YOUR PROFESSOR

If you're lucky enough to go to a school where you have access to your professors and T.A.s, you shouldn't feel hesitant about approaching them to talk about your paper. It's helpful to meet with your professor or T.A. at any stage of the writing process, but it's usually best to do it after you finish your outline. That way you can hear your professor's comments on your thesis and your arguments, without having already committed your ideas to paper.

Some professors and T.A.s are unwilling to read preliminary drafts, but they'll almost certainly listen to an informal summary of your arguments. Most of them actually enjoy this kind of interaction with students and will be thrilled to talk to you.

"Always meet with your professor. It really helps to discuss your ideas with someone else. They almost always want to help, and it's always a good idea."

**English major,
Carleton College '04**

writing your paper

If you have a strong thesis and a rough plan for how to lay out the main parts of your paper, actually writing it should be relatively easy. Keep track of your timeline, take breaks, and don't worry too much about style as you begin to write. You'll have a chance to revise and edit later—unless you're writing your paper the night before it's due.

Keep in mind that writing will probably lead to new ideas, or at least to altering your original thoughts. When we write we become involved with the material and can see issues in a different way from when we're just thinking about them. Don't be afraid to change an argument or supporting details as you write if you think doing so will improve your paper.

LEAVE YOURSELF TIME TO WRITE
▼

WRITE FOR AN AUDIENCE
▼

BE AWARE OF YOUR DISCIPLINE
▼

WRITE YOUR INTRODUCTION TWICE
▼

PAY ATTENTION TO TRANSITIONS
▼

USE QUOTES EFFECTIVELY
▼

DON'T PLAGIARIZE
▼

WRITE WITH STYLE
▼

END ON A GOOD NOTE
▼

TAKE BREAKS AS YOU WRITE

LEAVE YOURSELF TIME TO WRITE

Obviously, you can't always write your papers as far in advance as you'd like. You're running around trying to juggle academics, extracurriculars, parties, friends, sleep, and whatever else you might have piled up on your plate. You absolutely don't have to finish your entire first draft two weeks before the paper is due. But if you start writing with some time ahead of you, you'll feel more in control and less anxious about getting it done on time.

As much as you try to plan your time, you'll probably end up writing most of your paper in the last few days before it's due. That's fine, but if at all possible, leave yourself more than one day to get it done.

Writing ahead of time also removes the sense of urgency— and sometimes, panic—that can make you want to reach the page limit as quickly as possible. You should feel like you have plenty of time to think about what you say.

Sit back, put on a good CD, and plunge into it.

"Generally I'll spend the first day going over my reference materials and formulating my thesis. Then the next 2 or 3 days I'll spend on the outline and quotes alone, before I begin writing even a single word of my first draft. Then the remaining 3 or 4 days I'll spend on my first and final drafts."

**Philosophy and Computer Science major,
Vassar College '04**

WRITE FOR AN AUDIENCE

As you write your paper, imagine an audience—a person who is going to read it and who needs to understand what you're writing about. This will help you write more clearly and in a way that best communicates your ideas. Sometimes we get very formal and use tons of big words in our papers so that we sound more academic. Big words are fine, but remember that your main goal is to produce an intelligent and clear paper.

Think of writing as just a bit more polished and formal than talking. There should be no "hmmms" or "ahas" in your paper, and you should not use contractions like "we're" or "I'm" unless it's an extremely informal paper. But there's no need to write long-winded sentences or show off your SAT vocabulary just for the sake of impressing the reader. Don't hesitate to use a word like "lugubrious" if it seems right to you and it fits into the context of your paper, not just because you think that you'll be the only one in your class to use it. Be smart, but don't go out of your way to sound like you are.

author's corner
▼
When I started writing papers in college, I assumed that I needed to write in a more sophisticated way. At the time, I thought this meant using lots of big words and long sentences. I thought it made my ideas sound more important if I wrote them in a heavily worked, difficult style.

There are two problems with this. One is that I sounded like an arrogant, bratty freshman. The other is that I

*sometimes got bogged down in my convoluted sentences
and lost track of my thesis, or worse, ended up arguing
something different than I intended.*

*I don't shy away from big words and long sentences if I
think they're absolutely necessary. On the other hand, I try
not to write them for cosmetic appeal. They aren't as pretty
as I used to think, anyway.*

▲

Most professors care about the content and clarity of your
paper much more than the number of four-syllable words
that you use. They want to see that you've grasped the
class material and that you can intelligently talk about it in
a paper. But some professors have idiosyncrasies that you
should know about and keep in mind as you write.

*"My philosophy professor required that all of us use
10 new words in each of our weekly papers. "New"
meant that we had to go to the dictionary and find
words we'd never heard of before and put them in
our papers. It seemed ridiculous and it was, but to
get a decent grade we had to do it."*

**College of Social Studies major,
Wesleyan University '98**

BE AWARE OF YOUR DISCIPLINE

"In high school, we learned to write one kind of analytical paper that carried us through pretty much any class. In college, you have to learn that each discipline has its own standards for writing."

**History major,
Columbia University '04**

Every academic discipline tends to have its own conventions for written work. As you read the books and articles you're assigned over the semester, try to figure out what these conventions are and follow them as much as you can in your papers.

In art history, for example, there is a stronger emphasis on visual description than in most other fields. Sometimes a discipline has special stylistic conventions. For example, in philosophy, it's not unusual to read a paper that begins, "In this paper, I will argue that..." In an English class, this kind of opening would probably be frowned upon.

You should find out if your professor expects you to follow any particular style or format in your paper. Professors in intro classes are usually much more flexible and don't expect you to have mastered every nuance of their academic discipline just yet. If your professor does require a certain format, make an effort to follow it.

At the same time, don't get too carried away with the idea that your paper needs to be written for a particular discipline. No matter what subject your paper is about, you'll still be expected to have a thesis, make clear arguments, and present your ideas in an effective and well-written way.

WRITE YOUR INTRODUCTION TWICE

We've all been there—sitting in front of a computer screen, the clock counting down precious minutes, and the cursor blinking impatiently at the top of a blank page. Beginning to write your paper can be tough, kind of like starting to run after standing still for a while—it's much harder to get going than to keep going.

To get passed the empty screen, try writing your introduction twice. The first time, just try to get something down on paper. Don't worry about how it sounds or if it works as the perfect introduction to your paper. It probably doesn't. After you finish your paper, go back and rewrite your introduction. You'll find that it's much easier to handle because your entire paper is laid out in your mind.

A good introduction catches the reader's interest, clearly states the paper's thesis, and briefly suggests what arguments and analyses you'll use to support your main claim. Although it doesn't have to be, your thesis is usually stated in the last sentence of your introduction. Most students prefer to put it last and use it as a launching pad for the rest of the paper.

The introduction is one of the most creative parts of your paper, and there is no formula for writing a good one. Try to be original, but don't be too gimmicky. Don't start with a fictional narrative unless you're really comfortable writing fiction. Begin with a quote if you want, but make sure that it's relevant to your topic and is there for a purpose.

Many of us learned the "funnel" model for the introduction in high school: It starts with a broad claim and moves to a clear and specific thesis statement. There's some validity to this idea. Especially on the first draft of your paper, it can help to start with some general ideas about your topic and move to the focus of your paper—your thesis.

Some students take the idea of a funnel way too seriously. We've heard a few professors joke about the "primordial ooze" introduction in first-year papers: "Since he emerged from the primordial ooze, man has always wondered about (insert topic here)..." This kind of introduction doesn't get you very far. Whatever general statements you write at the beginning of your introduction, make sure that they're related to your topic and that you use them to set up your thesis.

PAY ATTENTION TO TRANSITIONS

"Topic sentences are a great way to organize a paper because they force you to view the work as a whole, with a logical progression from start to finish. Think of the topic sentences as bones in the skeleton of the paper. Don't just start writing paragraphs as they come to you, or you'll end up with quite a disfigured body."

**Journalism and Political Science major,
Northwestern University '04**

Disclaimer: If you think for a moment that you hear your high school English teacher talking, you're not entirely wrong. Most likely, all of our English teachers harped about transitions between sections and paragraphs. It turns out that they did it for a reason—a lack of good transitions in your paper can confuse your professor and cause him or her to not understand or misinterpret the logic and flow of your arguments.

Transitions are important because they explain to your reader how each part of your paper is connected to the others, and they give him or her a sense of direction for what's to come. Good transitions will make your paper read much easier and your professor will be able to actually think about what you're saying rather than try to get oriented in your paper.

Begin each paragraph with a transition that links it to the one preceding it. You may have learned lists of transition words in high school (words like "however," "therefore," and "furthermore"). Make friends with these words as you write, but make sure that your transitions don't all sound too similar or repetitive.

Here's one example of a good first transition sentence in a paragraph:

> The lack of equality between the lovers apparent in Browning's poem "Porphyria's Lover" contrasts with the relative equality we find between the loved and the beloved in his "Two in the Campagna."

The first part of the sentence likely links the new paragraph to the one before it. The sentence also gives us some sense of what this paragraph will be about. It seems like the writer has just discussed the relationship of the lovers in "Porphyria's Lover" and will begin to analyze the relationship in "Two in the Campagna." As readers, we know where we've been and where we're going.

Your first sentences don't need to be this formal. But they should connect each paragraph to the one before it and capture, at least in part, the main point that you're about to discuss.

USE QUOTES EFFECTIVELY

"Quotes are like the evidence a lawyer presents to a judge. They are the only concrete things you have. You should use them to support your arguments."

**History major,
Cornell University '04**

Many papers you write in college will require you to include quotes from one or more sources. Even if you don't have to do it, integrating a few quotes into your writing can add life and persuasiveness to your arguments. The key is to use quotes to support a point you're trying to make rather than just include them to fill space.

There are a few simple ways to use quotes in your paper. The first is not to quote at all and instead summarize the main points of a source. This approach works well for sources where the particular language of the quote is not especially important. If you're writing about history, paraphrasing is sometimes a great way to use secondary materials (the work of other historians and scholars) in your paper.

Another way to use source material is to quote a key word, phrase, or sentence that captures the essence of the text you're writing about. For example, if your paper is an attempt to explain the popularity of George W. Bush, and you're quoting a book by a very liberal writer, you might use the phrases "dynastic succession" and "crack monkey" in your paper. Carefully chosen words and phrases can really bring out your own arguments.

A third way to use quotes is to quote directly a whole block of text. These are called block-quotes and are usually single-spaced, placed in smaller font, and indented from the margins of the page. These are useful if there is a very rich passage in a source that is essential to your argument.

Make sure to connect quotes to your own arguments and to use each one to make your own points stronger. Analyze each quote you include, explain why it's significant and how it affects your own point. Professors hate seeing a bunch of quotes in a paper without understanding why they're there or what you intend to do with them beyond filling some space. Don't fall into this trap.

You should also make sure that the phrases and sentences you quote from other sources fit grammatically into your prose. For example:

> *The Backstreet Boys were an oasis in the cultural desert that was the late nineteen-nineties. Always modest, they never bragged about the impact they had on the development of a whole new genre of boy band music. In an MTV interview, they said that they merely hoped to "making beautiful songs."*

See the problem? The writer didn't adjust the quote to fit grammatically into the last sentence. The quote should have been adjusted to read:

They merely hoped to "mak[e] beautiful songs."

Use brackets to change verb tenses and clarify ambiguous pronouns (an undefined "he" or "she"). You can also adjust your own sentences to better align with the quotes. Whatever you do, make sure that you use quotes in a way that works grammatically with the rest of the sentence.

DON'T PLAGIARIZE

Plagiarism is passing off someone else's words or ideas as your own. We've probably heard about it since kindergarten, and we'll hear about it forever because it never goes away. People, including college students, continue to plagiarize—from books, articles, and from each other—and although some get caught, many more get away with it. But what fun is that, knowing that the "A" you got on your paper was not for you, but for the author of the paper you found on the Internet?

We won't preach about the moral issues of plagiarism, although there are many. And we won't remind you more than once that your own conscience will probably eat away at you if you blatantly plagiarize. Sticking to our mission of providing you with only the most practical and relevant information, we'll mention a few practical reasons not to plagiarize.

You can get caught, most definitely. T.A.s and professors have spent years reading through books, articles, and other papers related to your class and, chances are, they'll recognize when you're plagiarizing. They'll also be able to sense if the level and style of your usual writing suddenly changes when you hand in your paper. Then you're in trouble—ranging from a low grade to getting kicked out of school, depending on how much you plagiarize and how strict your school is. Don't do it.

On the flip side, you want to avoid being wrongly accused of plagiarism by carefully citing all of your sources. Find out what kind of citation system your professor prefers and use it. You don't need to put in citations for general knowledge: Uncontested dates, the authors of major works of literature, and basic historical facts don't need citations, for example. Anything else that's not your own work needs a citation. If you're not sure, cite the source anyway. It's better to have a few unnecessary footnotes than be accused of plagiarism.

One final reason not to plagiarize: You don't need to do it. You're smart enough and able enough to have great thoughts on your own. Why would you need to steal someone else's?

A NOTE ON INTERNET PAPER SERVICES

Yup, you can get a college paper from the Internet. Numerous paper depositories have sprung up in the last few years offering you A+ papers on any topic and for any class. All you have to do is fork over a few bucks and you're done with your paper assignment. Easy, right?

Not really. First of all, how do you know that the papers offered by these services are any good? You don't know and you have no way of finding out. Why would you trust someone else to write a better paper than you could if you have no idea about who the author is?

More importantly, however, if you bought a paper from one of these Internet services and turned it in as your own, you'd be plagiarizing big time.

Some students say that they check out Internet paper services to get ideas about how other people have approached similar topics. This doesn't sound so bad. But the temptation to plagiarize from the paper you're reading can be too great if you like what you see—it's right in front of you, you have two days to write your paper, you have another final in a day, and it would be so easy just to copy whole sections from someone else's paper.

Have some faith in yourself and leave Internet papers to someone else. You're smart enough to write your own.

WRITE WITH STYLE

You'll do fine on your paper if you have a strong thesis and your supporting arguments and points are well organized and clearly expressed. But to really ace it you should try to make your writing style distinctive in some way.

Learning to write with style is nothing any of us can learn to do overnight, but developing a distinctive personal style in your papers is not a bad goal to have as you write more of them. Reading great books and well-written magazine articles can help you improve your own writing style if it's something you're thinking about as you read.

Learning to write with flair—in a way that presents your ideas clearly but not in a dull academic tone—is worth a shot. You'd be surprised how far it can get you.

END ON A GOOD NOTE

In high school, you may have learned that the conclusion is a summary of your thesis followed by a brief explanation of the broader relevance of your arguments.

This basic structure is useful, so keep it in mind. You should try to encapsulate the overall thrust of your main argument or analysis in your conclusion. Don't give a long-winded summary of every major point you discussed in your paper, but try to remind your reader of your thesis and its key supporting arguments.

It can sometimes be useful to think of what your thesis implies about a particular work of literature, a particular time period, or a particular person that you wrote about. But if you write about the "broader relevance" of your topic, try not to get too carried away. Stick to your topic. Human nature, the cosmos, reality, and the nature of history are all favorite topics for some of the most uninteresting and trite conclusions.

Even if it sounds great at three in the morning on the day you're handing in your paper, don't write something like: "The debate on this topic will continue for the rest of human history." It doesn't say very much.

Have some fun with your conclusion and try to be a bit creative. It's a good place to use some appropriate humor or make a subtle point that's outside the scope of your paper. There's no need to be overly profound or clever, and if you can make your professor smile or pause to think for a moment, you'll leave a good last impression.

"In your conclusion, try to avoid repeating what you've already said. And ask yourself, so what? Why would anyone want to read this paper?"

**English Major,
Carleton College '04**

TAKE BREAKS AS YOU WRITE

Try to take a few breaks as you write. Our brains get tired, and when they're tired they tend not to be as sharp—ever read what you wrote after hours of writing and not know what in the world you meant by it?

Give yourself some room to breath. Get away from your paper—even if it's just for a few minutes—and you'll have more mental energy when you begin to work on it again.

writing notes

revising and editing your paper

Even if you only have a few hours before you have to hand in your paper, try to revise it at least once. Print out your first draft, get away from your computer, and read your paper with as much of an independent and critical eye as you can. Make sure that your ideas and arguments make sense, that they're presented in the most effective order, and then comb through your paper looking for spelling and grammar errors. Over and over we hear professors get annoyed at papers that have great content but are poorly edited.

The hard part is over. You've got your first draft on paper and the blank computer screen with your impatient cursor is no more. Put some extra effort into revising and editing your paper and you'll avoid getting a lower grade for something you worked hard to get right.

DO SOME MENTAL YOGA

▼

HAVE SOMEONE ELSE READ YOUR PAPER

▼

CHECK YOUR THESIS AND MAIN ARGUMENTS

▼

USE THE PASSIVE VOICE SPARINGLY

▼

SPICE UP YOUR SENTENCES

▼

DON'T KISS UP TO THE AUTHOR

▼

TAKE CARE OF THE SMALL STUFF

DO SOME MENTAL YOGA

"One of the most ineffective ways to revise a paper is to start making corrections and moving around material right after you finish your conclusion. You need a fresh pair of eyes to really get somewhat of an objective perspective on something you've just spent hours staring at. Take a break, even if it means coming back to it tomorrow."

Journalism and Political Science major, Northwestern University '04

Even if it's the night before your paper is due, you should try to take some time to step away from your keyboard. If you try to revise too soon, you won't be a very critical reader. If at all possible, you need to put some space and time between your mind and your paper.

Play Monopoly, go for a walk, watch TV, have a water balloon fight, eat a cookie. Do anything that isn't related to school or to your paper.

Once you feel more relaxed and refreshed, carefully read and re-read your paper. Print it out and write notes on it as you revise. Looking at something on the screen is not the same as holding it in your hand.

As your read, try to be methodical. Read your paper at least twice—once to get a sense of the overall content and flow and a second time to look for spelling and grammar problems. When you come across something you need to change, don't run to your computer right away. Take time to let it sink in before you start deleting whole paragraphs.

HAVE SOMEONE ELSE READ YOUR PAPER

You should strongly consider having someone else read a draft of your paper. Because you've spent so much time planning and writing it, you aren't the most critical judge of its flaws. Give it to someone whose opinion you trust, and who will take the time to read it carefully. Ask a friend, or take it to your school's writing center or workshop.

The writing centers at most schools are great resources and the students who work there have a lot of experience looking at student papers. Plus, unlike your roommate, they don't have to sleep ten feet from you for the next eight months. They have no reason to try to be nice rather than critical.

Ask your reader if he or she can follow your thesis and main arguments and analyses. Do they make sense or is something confusing? Can your reader tell you what your thesis is after reading the introduction? Do your arguments seem well organized?

Listen carefully to the feedback you hear and try not to be too defensive. At the same time, don't necessarily assume that your reader is right and you're wrong. If it's a subjective point—your reader thinks that your thesis is too contentious or that your second argument should go before your first, for example—there can be different ways to approach it. Think about the comments you get on your paper, evaluate them, and stick to your instincts if you really think that you've got the right approach.

CHECK YOUR THESIS AND MAIN ARGUMENTS

Look at your thesis and your core arguments. Now is the time to ask yourself if your thesis and your paper make the same point. If they don't, check to see if perhaps you reached a different conclusion by the time you finished your writing. Sometimes we start writing and arguing a certain point, but as we think about it and write more, we end up developing an argument for a slightly different one—or a drastically different one, in some cases. If you see a shift of focus in your paper as you revise, think for a moment whether you might need to alter your original thesis.

It might help to write out your original thesis statement out on a separate piece of paper and refer to it as you read through your first draft. That way, you'll always have it in front of you and can easily judge if your paper is going in a different direction.

USE THE PASSIVE VOICE SPARINGLY

Here's another "this sounds like my high school English teacher" piece of advice: Don't use too much of the passive voice in your paper.

The passive voice is a combination of a form of the verb "to be" (is, was) and a verb.

The active voice eliminates the "to be" verb and places the verb in the past, present, or future tense. In other words:

PASSIVE: was running/were being chased

*Biff **was running** from the giant poodle.*

*The Backstreet Boys **were being chased** by giant poodles.*

ACTIVE: ran/chased

*Biff **ran** from the giant poodle.*

*Giant poodles **chased** the Backstreet Boys.*

It's not necessarily wrong to use the passive voice. Sometimes it works and might be the only way to make a point. But in general, stick to its active counterpart. It makes your writing sound powerful and more direct. The active voice is easier to understand and more clearly expresses your point. Many professors say that the passive voice sounds more abstract and tentative, and abstract and tentative is not what you want to sound like in your college papers.

> *"I think people sometimes overcompensate by avoiding the passive voice completely. Focus on varying your sentence structure instead."*
>
> **English major,
> Carleton College '04**

SPICE UP YOUR SENTENCES

"I used the word "indeed" 15 times in one of my papers. The paper was four pages long. It was an obsession that I had to kick, but it wasn't easy. Once you like a word it just seems to type itself on the keyboard."

**College of Social Studies major,
Wesleyan University '98**

In the same way that most of us talk in recognizable speech patterns, we tend to fall into patterns in our writing. Some of us write a lot of long, winding sentences. Others tend to write short, choppy sentences. Some of us tend to overuse qualifications like "but" and "however," while others don't use them enough.

Read your paper and make sure that your sentences don't all sound alike.

• Do you use the same words again and again?

• Do you start every sentence with a preposition?

• Do you use the word "however" in the first sentence of every paragraph?

• Do you use the word "holistic" on every page?

Some consistency of style is important because it leads to a distinctive, personal voice. Without making your writing too inconstant, though, you should try to vary your sentence structure. Mix longer sentences with shorter ones. Look for repetitive words and substitute different ones. Make your writing interesting to read and your professor will breeze through your paper rather than become bored by it.

author's corner
▼

In my papers, I have a tendency to write really long sentences. When I'm revising my writing, I look carefully for places where I write too many of them in a row. If a section seems difficult to understand, I add a short sentence, or rewrite parts of the paragraph to include one or two short sentences. I had an English teacher in high school who told me to "punctuate my prose" with short sentences. That's not a rule that I hold to all the time, but it sometimes helps to make my writing sound more direct and forceful.
▲

DON'T KISS UP TO THE AUTHOR

Even if your paper is about *Hamlet*, you shouldn't go out of your way to flatter the author. No matter how much you adore Shakespeare, don't start off by saying, "As the greatest genius to ever write in the English language, Shakespeare has tremendous insight into the nature of human grief." Even if most people agree that Shakespeare is unparalleled, it sounds a bit pretentious to write this in your paper.

Some professors dislike these kinds of statements because they can sound like attempts to win brownie points. By kissing up to the author, it can seem like you're kissing up to the professor. You can also create the impression that you're trying to make up for other deficiencies in your paper by saying how much you loved the material on which it's based.

This doesn't mean that all flattery is out of the question. Just make sure not to overdo it, and that when you flatter, it's for some reason that's related to your paper.

TAKE CARE OF THE SMALL STUFF

Most professors are probably more interested in the quality of your writing and your ideas than technical perfection. As you revise, first spend time polishing the content of your paper before you spend hours working on mechanics.

On the other hand, all professors appreciate writing that's technically correct. Many of the papers they read are full of typos, spelling errors, and bad grammar. If you take the time to carefully proofread your paper, your professor will be impressed and won't be distracted from your ideas and arguments.

Read through your paper once to focus on grammar and spelling. Look for minor errors of all kinds—misplaced commas, un-capitalized names, and incomplete sentences—and make changes. Be sure to double-check the spelling of the author's names and titles of the works that you cite in your paper.

You've heard this before, of course, but here's a friendly reminder: Don't rely on your computer's spell- or grammar-check to catch all errors. It will find and fix some glaring errors, but it can't tell where you mean to say "there" vs. "their." Only your own eyes can catch word usage problems, so read through your paper carefully.

For details on proper grammar and word usage, please see the books listed in the "**helpful resources**" section. They can provide much more extensive help than we're qualified to present.

Before you hand in your paper and sigh with relief, quickly check to make sure that your pages are numbered, your name and paper title are on the first page, and that you staple your pages in the correct order.

Phew, now sigh with relief!

author's corner
▼

I was on campus after finals for a few days during my sophomore year, and I asked one of my professors if I could meet with him to discuss my final paper. I had spent probably over forty hours on it, including research, planning, and writing. By the time I turned it in, it had grown to almost thirty pages.

I was very interested to hear my professor's comments, partly because the paper was so long, and partly because it would be my only formal grade in the class for the entire semester. When I walked in to his office, I'm sure that I was visibly nervous. (I look nervous most of the time, so I probably looked absolutely terrified.)

It's easy to swallow a bad grade on a paper in the relative anonymity of a classroom, but it's a little more uncomfortable to read through thirty pages covered in red when your professor stares at you through his tortoise-shell glasses.

Despite my best efforts at proofreading, I noticed quickly that I had misspelled the name of the city that I was writing about consistently for at least half the paper. Additionally, I misspelled the name of one of my primary sources every time I used it.

He took my sloppiness as a personal affront. We had developed a good relationship over the previous semester, and he had given me lots of valuable advice as I worked toward a thesis. He had even given me a book at the end of the semester as a way of acknowledging my hard work on this paper. Fortunately, he understood that I was so burned out by the time I finished the paper that I simply didn't see the mistakes in my final draft.

▲

revising and editing notes

_____

_____

_____

_____

_____

_____

_____

_____

_____

_____

_____

_____

_____

_____

approaching a research paper

Some college papers require that you conduct independent research outside of class materials. These papers can be a bit more difficult to write because they require you to say something original about something you have to learn on your own. In general, though, a research paper is quite similar to any other paper in that it has a central thesis you have to support with evidence you find in your research. If you can tackle a regular college paper, you can tackle a research one.

Check out the following sections for some specific tips and advice about approaching a research paper.

CHOOSE A DOABLE TOPIC
▼

ROLL WITH THE PUNCHES
▼

RESEARCH FOR A PURPOSE
▼

READ THE BORING STUFF
▼

KEEP GOOD RECORDS
▼

BE CREATIVE ABOUT FINDING SOURCES
▼

HAVE A PLAN OF ATTACK FOR EACH SOURCE
▼

USE AN OUTLINE
▼

WRITE FROM BOOKS, NOT THE OUTLINE

CHOOSE A DOABLE TOPIC

When choosing a topic for your research paper, keep in mind that you'll need to have access to enough materials to complete your research in a limited amount of time. Choosing an amazingly interesting topic will do you no good if you can't find enough sources to do thorough research.

To know whether you can tackle your topic with enough resources, do some preliminary research before you really settle on it. Run a few searches on your library's computer catalog. See how many books on your topic you can find, and read a few chapters out of them.

Keep in mind that you can get access to a tremendous number of resources by using the Internet. Many newspaper and magazine articles are now available online and a few Internet libraries allow you to access whole books on your screen (www.questia.com and www.ebrary.com are the two most popular ones, and we talk a bit more about them in the "**helpful resources**" section).

You want to make sure that you can adequately research your topic without going crazy looking for sources and having to make arguments without enough supporting evidence. Put in some effort before settling on your final topic and you'll probably save yourself a great deal of frustration later on.

ROLL WITH THE PUNCHES

If you're writing a research paper on a somewhat unfamiliar topic, you might discover ideas in your research that you hadn't initially anticipated. Unlike papers based on materials you've read already, you won't know what you're getting yourself into when you start your research. Keep an open mind and be willing to change the direction of your paper as you dive deeper into your research.

In fact, you should expect your topic to evolve as you read. That's the point of research—to learn about a particular topic in detail and figure out exactly what you want to say about it.

RESEARCH FOR A PURPOSE

Researching can actually be really fun and you might find yourself completely engrossed in reading about the art of the Javanese Gamelan. (No, really.) It can be easy to lose your sense of direction and purpose in your research and to end up having researched some pretty interesting but irrelevant information for your paper. If you had all the time in the world, that would be just fine. But you're in college and you're busy, so you need to research for a purpose.

The purpose of your research is to find evidence to support the main arguments of your paper and your thesis.

Before you dive head first into your research, take a moment and think about your topic. Chances are, you know something about it already. Can your formulate a preliminary thesis? You might want to read through the first few sources you've gathered and then jot down some ideas. Your thesis doesn't have to be great at this point, but it will help to actually have a direction as you begin to research and look for more sources.

At the same time, make sure that you're flexible as you research and don't stay too wedded to your initial thesis. Remember that it was just an initial idea to give you direction and it can change significantly as you research and find evidence that either supports your initial position or argues against it. Try to keep as much of an objective mindset as you can when you research, and be open to learning things that you hadn't anticipated.

READ THE BORING STUFF

When you start compiling sources for your paper, you should make an effort to read the footnotes and bibliographies of the sources that you find most useful. Nobody likes reading bibliographies, but if you do, you'll get a much better idea of other sources you should consider. You'll save yourself a lot of time trying to find related sources using your library's card catalogue or searching on the Internet.

KEEP GOOD RECORDS

It's really important to keep good notes as you research. Your mind might be brilliant and remember everything now, but things have a tendency to fade with time. You can save yourself a lot of anxiety and frustration later on if you write down the important ideas and specific points now.

Make sure to write down the most significant points that you find in each source, the corresponding page numbers, and the exact name of the source. Use Post-It notes to mark important passages in books and articles.

If you keep good records, you'll be able to organize your notes as you make your outline. You'll also avoid plagiarizing—by having a clear record of where your ideas came from. It can be very easy to absorb ideas from one source and think they're your own.

author's corner
▼
Last year, I had to write my first big research paper, a thirty-page beast of an assignment. I had never used notes for a research paper before, and I didn't think that I would ever need to. At first this worked out fine, but as I got to my twentieth book about commerce in South India in the sixteenth century, my mind was a blur. Somehow, I managed to pull together something halfway decent for my final paper, but it took much longer than it should have. I spent more time sifting through books than I did writing my paper. I would spent fifteen minutes looking for one passage that I needed and another ten minutes re-reading what I'd already read.
▲

BE CREATIVE ABOUT FINDING SOURCES

Be really creative about finding useful and unique sources for your paper. See if you can find organizations related to your topic and scour their discussions, reading lists, reports, and other data. Many conferences now post their discussions and presentations online as well. Find those that are relevant and get a hold of the materials.

Remember also that the sources you'll be using won't always be in print form. There may have been a great documentary film on the topic, a radio show, or a symposium. Check out these sources—you can find some unique information to really improve the quality of your paper and your professor will be impressed.

Also remember that your professor is a great resource for helping you with your research. He or she has probably read a lot of material on your topic and can suggest where you should look.

HAVE A PLAN OF ATTACK FOR EACH SOURCE

Chances are, you're not going to have enough time, patience, or interest to read through each of your sources in detail. And there's really no need to do this. What you do need to do is find information in your research that reveals something about your topic and your thesis.

With this in mind, there will be many sources from which you read just a few pages, or even just a paragraph. To make sure that you can find the critical information without wasting time, develop a system for how you'll work with each source. Here are a few suggestions:

- Check the book's table of contents to find the most relevant sections.

- Skim through the introduction. This is usually the roadmap to the book or article, and it will help you focus on the source's key sections.

- After you find relevant chapters or sections, read them and take notes. Write down enough information so that it will make sense to you when you read it later, but avoid taking down sentences word for word.

- Check out the footnotes in the relevant sections and the bibliography as discussed earlier.

You can use these steps as your guidelines and add your own, but just remember to have a plan of attack for each source rather than spending your valuable time browsing through pages after pages without a clear direction.

A NOTE ON PRIMARY VS. SECONDARY SOURCES

Primary sources are those created and left behind by the participants of historical events, such as letters, diaries, manuscripts, and newspaper articles written at the time of these events. Primary sources allow you, the researcher, to get as close to these historical events as possible, and to formulate your own conclusions about them.

As you research, you should aim to locate as many primary sources related to your topic as possible. Depending on your topic, primary sources may be plentiful or scarce, but you should do the legwork necessary to find them. In some courses, your professors might even require that you cite a certain number of primary sources.

Secondary sources are interpretations of primary sources created after certain events took place. A history textbook is a great example of a secondary source. Milk secondary sources for what they're worth—great syntheses of information, summaries of analyses, and opinions on particular topics.

USE AN OUTLINE

Even more than for other papers, an outline is a vital tool for writing good research papers. It's a way to summarize and consolidate your research into logical and clear arguments.

As we've already mentioned, don't use your outline to write down every point that you'll address in your paper. Use it to plan the structure of your paper and the general shape and flow of your arguments.

WRITE FROM BOOKS, NOT THE OUTLINE

As you write your paper, don't forget to refer to your sources. Often. If you write just from your outline, your notes, and your memory you risk missing important points and nuances. Your outline should remind you of where you are in your paper and where you're headed, but you should try not to substitute it entirely for your sources.

Surround yourself with the books that you used to generate your outline, and reference them as you write. Your paper will be richer and you'll be able to find great quotes or passages to give life to your arguments.

research paper notes

the daily grind

Writing papers is something that most of us do a lot in college. It's like a rite of passage, and a painful one at times. As you go through the experience, keep a few things in mind to stay sane and to keep writing.

▶ BE FLEXIBLE

If there's one theme to this guide, it's that writing can't be boiled down to just one simple procedure. There are steps you can take to help you write a better paper, but there isn't one process that will generate a good paper for everyone.

Be flexible, be creative, and find a way to write that works for you. If you find that the way you approached your first paper doesn't work, you should change your approach for your second one. If you have just a few hours to write a paper, be flexible enough to figure out how to make it work and still follow some key principles. Trust yourself to find a way to write that works for you.

▶ PACE YOURSELF

Especially for your first few papers, leave yourself some time to get into your writing groove and get them done well. Don't feel like you have to get everything finished in one sitting. Just because your roommate can sit down at her computer and bang out a ten-page draft of her paper doesn't mean that you should try to do the same.

Take your time to think through your topic, your thesis, and how you will structure your paper. If you feel anxious and rushed, you'll have a harder time getting your thoughts in order and down on paper.

▶ DON'T GET DISCOURAGED

Writing doesn't come naturally to everyone. Actually, writing probably doesn't come naturally to most people. Give yourself some room to learn how to write for college and try not to get discouraged if you don't do well on your first few papers. Many of us get through high school without having to write more than one or two papers along the way, so we really don't have much experience to learn from.

Try to remember that if you do poorly on your first paper, it doesn't mean that you're stupid or a bad writer. It just means that you did poorly on your first paper. Figure out what went wrong and work to fix it. No one is expecting you to ace everything right away, not even your professors.

▶ GET HELP WHEN YOU NEED IT

Don't be afraid to ask for help when you need it. Go talk to your professor. Go to the writing center. Talk to a friend who seems to ace every paper.

Even if you don't have anything concrete to talk about and you just want to bounce some ideas off someone, you shouldn't hide out in your room. Professors and T.A.s are always happy to talk to students during office hours, and they'll probably make time to see you at other times as well. Asking them for help doesn't make you look stupid—quite the opposite, in fact.

Don't be afraid to have someone else read your writing. After all, that's what writing is for.

▶ BE GUTSY

Take some chances in your paper.

Come up with an unconventional thesis.

Research a unique topic that hasn't been researched a hundred times over.

Do some outside research for a paper that doesn't require it.

Chuck a paragraph—or five—in your paper if it doesn't make sense to you as you revise.

You don't have to hate writing papers, and since you have to write them anyway, try to have some fun!

what "they" say

We asked. They answered. Here are a few pieces of advice from professors and writing workshop directors from Dartmouth, Oberlin, Princeton, and Williams. Since your own professors probably share a few of their opinions, it might be good to keep these in mind as you write.

WHAT IS THE ONE PIECE OF ADVICE YOU WOULD GIVE TO STUDENTS ABOUT WRITING?

"First advice: Be able to summarize the paper in a single statement or question, paying attention to the predicate.

Second advice: read The Elements of Style, *by Strunk and White, pp. 15-33."*

"Have an argument to make. A college paper is not (only) a way of proving you did the work, read the book, know the stuff. It's a way of making the material of the course your own by entering into a vital and substantive discussion/ debate of it."

"Learn the territory. Spend some time getting to know what "makes" an academic paper. And remember that your paper should pass the "So what?" test. Craft an argument worth reading, and craft it with care."

"You can't write a really thoughtful paper the night before it's due. I know you think you can; everyone thinks they can. But it's not true. Good writing is inseparable from good thinking, and good thinking takes time. If you have been thinking about your paper for a week—well, then you may be able to sit down and write it the night before."

WHERE DO YOU THINK MOST STUDENTS GO WRONG WHEN WRITING THEIR FIRST PAPER IN COLLEGE?

"Both before they begin to write and as they're writing, some students don't keep track of the statement they're trying to make or the question they're trying to answer. They should refer to a written version of it at all times."

"Students often misjudge the audience's expectations. Many believe that they have to write to please the professor, so they simply repeat all the brilliant things that the prof has already said in class. Or they inflate their prose, using as many abstract nouns as they can. Or they simply don't spend enough time thinking the matter through. And finally, they don't allow themselves time enough to revise."

"The problem is what DOESN'T happen before students even begin to write. Some students think that writing a paper is somehow a discrete act, when writing a paper is really just the process by which they communicate all the thinking and knowledge-acquisition that has already gone on. Before writing, there has to be reading, and note taking, and talking, and percolating. Then you have a reason to write."

WHAT CAN STUDENTS DO TO IMPROVE THEIR WRITING OVER THE LONG TERM?

"Write more papers. Edit what you've written."

"Revise! A first draft is very often a way of finding out what you want to argue. Once you've gotten there, you need to go back and figure out what is the best strategy for presenting the argument you want to make."

helpful resources

Before you turn to writing manuals or other helpful resources, make sure to take advantage of the writing resources your school already offers. Writing workshops, your professors, and T.A.s are all invaluable—not to mention easily accessible and free—resources, and you should get as much help from them as you need.

What we've tried to do in this section is suggest a few books and websites that you can turn to, for help with specific issues like research, grammar, and general language usage.

BOOKS

The Elements of Style, by William Strunk Jr., E.B. White, Charles Osgood, and Roger Angell. Allyn & Bacon, 4th Edition, 2000.

The classic. If you haven't read it yet, you should read it cover to cover. It has more useful ideas about writing in a more accessible format than just about any other book available. It's the kind of book you'll have on your shelf for the rest of your life.

Woe Is I, by Patricia T. O'Connor. G.P. Putnam's Sons, 1996.

This book gives the clearest and most useful summary of English usage that you'll find anywhere. It's very readable, and you might actually laugh as you read about pronouns. It may turn you into a huge grammar geek.

The Chicago Manual of Style: The Essential Guide for Writers, Editors and Publishers, by John Grossman (Preface). University of Chicago Press, 14th Edition, 1993.

Use this book for information on grammar, usage, and style. It's also probably the most extensive resource for citation formats. Refer to it often as you write research papers to make sure that you use proper academic formatting.

WEBSITES

www.dictionary.com

A useful and easy-to-remember website that you can use to check the definitions of words as you write. The definitions aren't always the most comprehensive, but they'll usually get the job done quickly.

www.questia.com

Questia claims to be the largest online library where—with an Internet connection and a few dollars per month—you can read through thousands of social science and humanities books, make notes, create footnotes and bibliographies, and never lose track of a single page. It can be pretty useful if you can find resources related to your topic.

See if you can get a free trial membership and check it out.

www.ebrary.com

Pretty much the same as Questia, but you might want to check it out because some sources that are available from one aren't always offered by the other.

www.thesaurus.com

An easy-to-use online version of the ever-necessary Roget's Thesaurus. You can search for synonyms by word or topic, just like in the book version. So if you don't feel like flipping pages, this is a great tool.

the final word

No matter how nervous you might be about writing your first few college papers, try not to write for the grade. Try to write to be convincing and to reveal something about a topic that others have not yet considered. Try to care about what you say. And try to enjoy it. Treat it as an experiment, not an exam.

When you finally hand in a copy of your paper to your professor, you should feel relieved and satisfied. No matter how you do on your first paper, it's a great feat just to get it done. You should be pretty proud of yourself.

You'll probably quickly forget what your first paper was about, or even what class you wrote it for. But it'll inevitably teach you something about yourself as a writer. And learning about yourself is part of why you came to college in the first place, right?

Good luck, and write on!

To learn more about **Students Helping Students™**
guides, read samples, share your own experiences with
other students, suggest a topic or ask questions, visit us at
www.studentshelpingstudents.com!